Meanwell

Janice Miller Potter

Poems Copyright © 2012 by Janice Miller Potter

All rights reserved. No part of this book may be reproduced in any form or by any means without the prior written consent of the publisher, except in the case of brief quotations used in reviews and certain other noncommercial uses permitted by copyright law.

.

ISBN-13: 978-1-937677-35-0
Library of Congress Control Number: 2012949889

Fomite
58 Peru Street
Burlington, VT 05401
www.fomitepress.com

Cover Art - Edwin Austin Abbey, "The Trial of Anne Hutchinson" (1901)
Author Photo - Heather Potter

Meanwell

For Richard, Dawn, and Heather

Acknowledgments

I am grateful for the lives of Anne Bradstreet (1612-1672) and Anne Hutchinson (1591-1643), two early American women of enduring courage and creativity.

As *Meanwell* evolved, I spent many hours with the following:

>Anne Bradstreet, *The Works of Anne Bradstreet*, edited by Jeannine Hensley, with a foreword by Adrienne Rich
>John Berryman, *Homage to Mistress Bradstreet*
>Helen Campbell, *Anne Bradstreet and Her Time*
>Charlotte Gordon, *Mistress Bradstreet: The Untold Life of America's First Poet*
>John Winthrop, *The Journal of John Winthrop*
>*The Examination of Mrs. Ann Hutchinson at the Court at Newtown (1637)*, court transcript

For permission to use woodcut illustrations by Thomas Bewick and his school, I acknowledge the generosity of the *Dover Pictorial Archive*.

The cover illustration of "Anne Hutchinson on Trial" (1901) is a reproduction of the art of Edwin Austin Abbey (1852-1911).

I wish to thank Marc Estrin and Donna Bister, editors and publishers of Fomite Press, for taking on *Meanwell* and for guiding me through the publication process with wisdom and kindness.

As always, I am thankful for the support and encouragement of my husband Richard and daughters Dawn and Heather.

Contents

A Knot of Sea 1
Who I Was and Where I Came From 2
Good Mistress Bradstreet 4
Those Obnoxious to Bishops Order Bed Matters Cast into the Sea 5
Jersey Guy Washes Away Sermons 6
The Death of a Lewd Seaman Attends a Sea-Born Child 7
From the Shore the Scent of a Garden Invisible to Mortals 11
Wild Strawberries 12
Worse Than A Stew Is Salem 13
I Must Kill the Hog Like It or Not 15
After Her Safe Delivery We Feast on Boiled Pork 16
In the Arms of Anne Hutchinson 17
All Political Huff We Remove to Ipswich 21
Paper Nights 23
The Trial of Anne Hutchinson 24
So To Number Our Days 27
When the Ministers Heard Anne Hutchinson Was Scalped 29
A Servant Drops a Lit Candle 31
Sagamore 37
Sister Death 39
Of Husbands and Step-Dames 40
Two Annes Have I Served Half-Faithfully 41
In Exile from Grave Illusion 44
Meanwell 46

WATER

A Knot of Sea

Ruined as I am the sea makes no mind
as it leaps and licks higher by the moment
with the icy winds that hound us
like dogs baring long teeth at our bellies
and where is our God I wonder
who would seem to punish the revolt
of dour Puritan men against the prelates
with slanderous blows of the great water
against ship's hull and landsmen's sanity
for all not fastened flies through the air
or slides across the boards like black works
of witches mayhap hidden in our hold

and I errant soul as I am I am called
time after time by the pious women laid
like sardines brined in the foul hold
puking over their waste-brown babes
as if a servant might possess a low power
to save souls from the monstrous jaws
of the watery beast that wing-spread doth
rise and bend over our whole company
which but for those affrighted ministers
praying for calm might for a twinkling
of a dark eye be frozen in mental craze
as the vast angel of the Lord guarding us

for still our filthy bilge swims the pure sea
despite the matter of the barreled cod
boughten by Mr. Winthrop to feed landsmen
perhaps to spruce up dried tongue in bran
though in such tempest only I hunger for salt
stiff winds freezing across the slantwise decks
so that I witness an enormous knot of sea
cast its weighty coils upon the fish prison
shattering oaken staves and spangling ice-spray
like jewels across decks swarming with cod
great muscled living missiles flipping free
meaning so well I shake laughter into the howl

Who I Was and Where I Came From

Few would think I were born in a castle
the truth be that I came
between washtubs and gentlemen's ruffs

for cook said my dame was a rude wench
in the Earl of Lincoln's rents
my sire a brandy-gentleman of some extract

this thought I may treasure with the year
sixteen hundred and twelve
that which the Countesse Elizabeth named

as the year of my trespass into earthly time
her slip of kindness
to the bairn of a wet-nurse sucked to death

for being a slut though she did mean well
thus out of charity was I
named Meanwell for my mother's intentions

so surely the Countesse wrote her *Nurserie*
to rally fine ladies to milk
their own breasts to save their babes' souls

but whether my mother was a book or not
I have no knowledge
other than that I was always without parent

among the throng of carnal servants kept
at Sempringham estate
plucking out hen-feathers and shelling peas

for of books I knew little except bindings
to tell which pen be
from the Countesse or from the Patriarchs

little I knew till they hired stern steward Dudley
to oversee the earl's estate
when in my eighth year like his sickly Anne I

was brought with hayseeds in my lank hair
to fetch and carry
the earl's musty old books to her sick-bed

where the dark-curled child lay smothered
within velvet draperies
sore-athirst while turning page after page

and I did marvel on this well-beloved child
whose dear mother Dorothy
wrapped her with her cherished book in arms

while my vexed eyes one blue and one brown
did cloud with desire
to seize her soft nest once sickness was done

Good Mistress Bradstreet

Still does she survive
        her brow of white limestone
                sculpted in its socket of Lincolnshire
look a tiny furrow is carving out
        a wrathful angel of protest against that screw her father Master Thomas Dudley
                as he splutters over them verily like
one of the precious ministers whose hides be likely spitted and hung like hogs
        one day for how they preach rebellion against King Charles
                but meanwhile keep us gadding
after the whereabouts of God who hides his face from England
        putting out our hearth-fires with damp decrees from the steward's lip
                that this home be lost to us
thus to market go cattle houses pretty tables and chairs while we women pack chests brimful
        of blankets linens dried out victualings that will groan overland to a ship
                and be shied across the sea like a shard of stone

see at this very moment
        a mote of spittle spinning on her tongue
                as if she would speak or cry out in pitiful anguish of loss
spying the corner in the ancient black oak
        cupboard where she hid the remnant of a flax doll for me who was meant by God
                to n'er do well but in lifting volumes of words for her poor eyes
I Meanwell hate her for the doting
        that adorns her through mother father brother sister even a husband
                for it's God's truth that perusing her brother's books she fell into carnal desire
for that stooge Bradstreet and he for her and so for that they were wed and I wondered
        at the ease of this carnal solution since what the cook said
                about my slut-mother who drowned in a ditch still rang in my ears
but at this moment the mote of spittle is
        spilling from her pink tongue that is slowly licking it dry as
                the heart that rose to burst rather than break a vow of obedience

Those Obnoxious to Bishops Order
Bed Matters Cast Into the Sea

Having hoisted up the barrels and hogsheads and chests
full to bursting with the domestic goods of the Dissenters
having hoisted up bawling cattle belted by their middles
high into the damp air and swinging them over the docks
onto the deck of the *Arbella* all slick hooves and wild eyes
for the lurching underneath never ceases to craze them

nothing further happens while we wait for stiffe winds
so that the listing ship casts anchor before Yarmouth where
Mr. Winthrop orders a fast for Friday the 2nd of April
nothing further happens till Monday when a skimpy maid
of Sir Tichard Saltonstall falls down a grate by the cook-room
and a nimble seaman catches her coarse-handed by the arse

on the 8th of April the ship weighs anchor as good winds
favor us at last and I hover close behind my Mistress Anne
while she crouches on the boards listening to the reverend
Phillips preach on the covenant of works that await us all
while I watch a seaman's firm buttock rise on the mizzen
and I do mean to heed but for a handsome gale in my ears

then those concerned men who were obnoxious to bishops
conceive that one spark might condemn all to punishing fires
therefore cause all manner of bed matters cast into the sea
while their shuddering good-wives watch salt-waves daggle
from crest to crest their precious woolen blankets and rugs
that color the grim cold sea till they sink slowly slowly

Jersey Guy Washes Away Sermons

As the rough sea licks our bitten skin with salt tongue
we lie half-smothered under its endless passion
and O how the pasty-faced minister attempts to arouse

the poor scurvy-ridden children from the green toils
of sea-sickness with a sermon on Eve's grievous fault
but only Mistress Dorothy thinks how to cure torment

by laying a rope like a tissue between males and females
which all together we lift up and down and up and down
our blood coursing with the steady rhythm of the waves

and O my Guy from Jersey I do so dream of your body
as it covered mine in Lincoln's black oak woods
and O my Guy de Poingdestre as you called yourself then

to think how you stowed your soft honey-brown cattle
across the Channel only that they be foully bound
to cross a worse swathe of sea and ice O my tutor my love

what for could I not learn your Frenchy words in Jerriais
and sail to the Isle of Jersey and not America
my Jersey Guy my fault I raise my rope and plunge it down

The Death of a Lewd Seaman Attends a Sea-Born Child

Heaving and setting with such force that the ocean might spill
from off God's earth makes it a great wonder
to behold our sister ship the painted *Jewel*
for we need her midwife most urgently to disencumber
a good-wife retching under her bloody cloak on the shit-slick boards
where fearful ladies huddle under the hatches from the storm

though I mean well I cannot bear to look on her
small head where a twist of hen-scrapings might be her face
for she appears not a creature of a human nature
rather the entrails of an animal gouged alive from its earthly form
the shrieks swelling over its foul-smelling mire
and though I would have hope I have none and climb to the sea

where with seamen and landsmen headed by Mr. Winthrop
I witness the *Jewel* riding not half a league off
with sails drawn as if in Puritan abstinence before the Lord
while lifting and plunging among the waves a shallop
ferries three stone-like figures of seamen who must soon
retrace the waves for the midwife now daft in a brandy-doze

but when twice-crossed waters calm a sea-born child breathes
the salt air of frigid ocean before the air of any nation
while his father and the ministers debate whether the ocean be
powerful enough for a baptism and my weak attention turns
to the voice of Mr. Winthrop intoning a gossip from the *Jewel*
that a seaman had perished but he was a very lewd fellow

AIR

From the Shore the Scent of a Garden Invisible to Mortals

Through weeks of gales and cold
we lamented our blankets lost among the fishes
as the rigging whistled and the ship shot through the waves
to places where porpoises leapt to our spears
and a great whale drifted along our side spouting water
as if it were God's leviathan sleepily smoking his pipe at twilight

I lurch about serving muddy beer and cold calf's-tongue
to my Master and Mistress Bradstreet who chew
with disgust as a sailor taunts them with his bawdy song
I drift among servants a-shiver on deck
where I marvel at our crude band of sufferers
for few mortals will witness the wonders of God's ocean

let alone with two-colored eyes
that might be condemned as a sign of witchcraft
should I lift them to the minister while he preaches on sin
therefore will I turn a brown eye on sailors playing the wags
with bedraggled children who tease the seamen
therefore will I avert a blue eye to the wave-trails on the horizon

when suddenly a pigeon thrashes the air
and settles at my feet and I am seized with rapture
at this miracle on the sunlit ocean upon the 8th of June
in jubilee I shout to my mistress that she may not miss the wild dove
when suddenly all of the servants begin to cry for joy as
there came a smell off the shore like the smell of a garden

Wild Strawberries

Where we dry our skirts
in the plummeting breeze
wild strawberries
sprout like holy manna
above the tide-mark
hairy-leaved and coarse-toothed
arrayed in white blossoms
and seedy white fruits
that ripen scarlet and crimson
before our cautious eyes

but we give in we give in
to ardors of starvation
falling on chapped knees
we pick the berries by handfuls
bruise them in our mouths
crush sharp fragrant juices
deep into our throats
no matter that one side
of every ripening fruit
is always rotten

Worse Than A Stew Is Salem

Near dawn on June 12th
a sailor sights isles of rock
in white-capped waters
and Puritans snivel aloud
like snot-nosed brats

the thankful captain fires
two cannon shots
as the stout *Arbella* passes
through a narrow strait
and draws its sails

within Plum Cove
where all Salem welcomes us
into the Kingdom
of Christ in the New World
with tears we believe

until on the beach
we meet the live skeletons
who have planted above eighty
in the northern snows
and have no corn nor bread

lice-bitten orphans beg us
for the victuals we ourselves
desperately require
and we must leave them to it
for above all

Mr. Winthrop and Mr. Dudley
are practical men
then Winthrop's boy drowns
and shuddering we flee by the rivers
Charles and Mystic

to Charlestown where
we husky maids sweat with the men
raising English wigwams
while those scurvy-faint ones
go ghostly loving and pitiful

worse than a stew is Salem
and Charlestown stinks of death and dung
if I were a dove I'd fly to green Lincoln
where surely my Guy of Jersey
auctions his doe-eyed young heifers

I Must Kill the Hog Like It or Not

In New Towne some call Cambridge
the Bradstreets' spotty fatte pigge
increases as leaves yellow into the fall
and Mistress Bradstreet fattens also
to our relief and delight for at last
we are kept awake by no sobbing prayers
with the bed-noises in the night

now while the fatte pigge broadens
my mistress boils up jellies and jams
and has even swiftly learned to wring
without qualm the necks of squawking fowl
and pull out their gizzards and unlaid eggs
for her servants do little she does not
except that her fatte pigge still will grow

till the strongest woman in the house
must one morning stab the poor pigge
who does so love its turnips and cabbages
and hold it close in her arms till all
its blood drains down to a pudding pan
and its pigge-soul flies squealing to heaven
like it or not I must kill the hog

After Her Safe Delivery We Feast on Boiled Pork

Such a heretic in my heart I am
that God shall damn me for my grief
for Mistress Bradstreet's fatte pigge
while she approaches her peril

perhaps the folly of my heart buys her
an ounce of earthly grace for surely
her own goodness and industry in advent
already purchase her heavenly salvation

with an excess of cheer she laid up
meates minces cheeses jellies apples pyes
for others during her travail to come
and afterward perhaps for her funeral

she has embroidered a christening shawl
of silk with pink roses and lace fringe
to dissuade death from taking her child
too soon from this Puritan vale of tears

and now nineteen wives fill her house
eating the pyes and swapping birth tales
while my poor mistress groans and cries
and I am hustled for linens and kettles

while my own soul is surely decayed
with mean envy and sorrow for the pigge
however on the birthing stool all women
must pay with pain for the sin of Eve

which I suppose I shall not do
but when my mistress expels a soppy boy
greedy for the air and she thrives in her joy
all that remains is to tell the men outside

how wondrously God has favored His Colony
in the New World and the father with a son
whose safe delivery means that now
we must feast on boiled pork with mince pyes

In the Arms of Anne Hutchinson

With my tattered soul sadly
on my guilty mind
I hear of the midwife
Anne Hutchinson
who preaches to crowds that
to be born woman is
to be blessed by God

this from one who
suffered for our Eve's sin
fourteen times
but steadfastly embraces
her sex as well as her husband
while the Puritan ministers
stew close to a boil

as wives and daughters flock
to female meetings
to hear this midwife-mother
skewer dogma on a pike
she calls her divine inspiration
at which I look up
and she takes me in her arms

FIRE

All Political Huff We Remove to Ipswich

Burnt once too often he thunders
with the flush of crimson around his ears
that marks some fiery faggot soon to explode
out of self-inflicted martyrdom
these are dangerous times when servants vanish
and the Dudley and the Bradstreet contingents fall silent

wainscoting he shouts too much show of adornment
he cries in fraudulent disbelief
for wainscoting a public censure by the high-and-mighty governor
so Winthrop and Dudley have fallen out
the flush darkens to the upshot of the matter
we must remove to Ipswich

no matter that it's late November
no matter that his daughter is breeding her second child
in any event she is not to have that Hutchinson woman again
he'll thumb his nose on Cambridge and Boston
and Bradstreet will do as he's told
it goes without saying that the servants are summoned for duty at once

with a shade of insolence I confess
we take the brunt of old Dudley's hot temper
sorting mending packing discarding hoisting rounding up
livestock we mutter that we may as well be dumb beasts too
too hardly used we make them ready
for our trek far north through a frost-bitten wilderness

to me lugging bundles her voice seems a brainless bit of fluff
panting on an Indian trail up hill and down dell
blabbing about the glistering sunlight and the stately oaks
and the inspiring power which appears on gazing at sun through dry leaves
but as I must keep one eye on the goods and another on the guides
treacherous Indians no doubt I would not know

but Dudley burnt once too often justifies
aches blisters flaming raw-red hands while psalms rise to God's handiwork
never mind build their fire cook their meal clear brush for their sleep
will it never end no we must guard their cows and pigs all night
and be fresh to conquer twenty miles of marsh tomorrow
after which Dudley and Bradstreet will lead us into cheering Ipswich

which turns out to be an ant-hill of books and scholars
Bradstreet's old college cronies who also crave
more Indian land and more distance from female disturbances
so it appears that once more I will convey volumes
and listen as her quill scripts divine inspiration and some line is read aloud
like her childhood book and sick-bed friend

Paper Nights

Nights in the gabled Agawam house
draw a shade thin as the scarce
paper for poems
she writes on nights when
sleep won't come or
she drives sleep from her bed
for the poems that come
blunting her agonies
with revelation

she yearns
to fill her urn of death
with the refuse of pleasure
wrappers of love spent
on that husband who surely never
got a single one of her poems
on her most honoured father
on seasons ages monarchies Sidney
her fanciful revered ancestor

she ought to turn
with a world of timely things
her birds hatched her plums and apples
ripened her corn and grass mown
compassionate women and pretty babes
in birthing-rooms life and death
in paper nights O God let her brittle words
come down to earth where
modest parsley and bay leaves grow

The Trial of Anne Hutchinson

       1.

Tending her flock of children and servants
during grim days that grind down into November
does my young Mistress Bradstreet
consider the plight of the midwife Anne Hutchinson
which is on the lips of every free and indentured soul

in the streets rawboned boys stage snow battles between
gangs called Grace and Works
I have it from the blacksmith's boy with a bloody ear
that Works put rocks in their balls

here in Ipswich at Agawam the women apostles declare
Mistress Hutchinson preaches more sense from a motion of the spirit
than any of your black-coates from the Ninneversity
and some ruffian-men caw like crows to the Reverend's face

but where is the plain-speaking Mistress Bradstreet
in all of this public crisis
        why silent as the great pyramids
in one of her mysterious monarchies I hear rhythmed every night
          how could it be otherwise
      Dudley her honoured father lights the wildfire

              heresy

     burning the bitter coasts of New England

       2.

November sky hangs low over the courtroom in Boston
                                     dull cold
     despite a throng of hundreds

magistrates ministers gentry in black with broad white ruffs and high-crowned hats
soldiers spruced and stiff in buff coats
yeomen and rabble in soiled homespun clothes

women defiantly garbed in bodices bright as the rainbow

the prisoner in the dock

Anne Hutchinson wraith-thin and heavy with her fifteenth child
forbidden food and counsel and made to stand for hours before
                the honourable magistrates

Winthrop Dudley Endicott Nowell Stoughton Bradstreet

              were I there I would wear scarlet

Winthrop opens with the general charge of heresy
but Anne Hutchinson demands he spell out what she denies to the death
so strong that Winthrop falls back the wind knocked out of him

ferocious Dudley attacks with a wrath that knows no bounds
calling to perjure themselves those black-coates Symmes Welde Wilson Peters
even the Rev. Soft-Reluctance Cotton libels her to save his own skin

Anne Hutchinson shoves their worthlessness up their long noses
allowing that Mr. Cotton alone holds thorough-furnishing for his vocation
at her turning the other cheek he reddens to the roots of his hair

grilling hours the judges prove only that Puritan ministers fear a superior woman
it is clear she cannot be convicted for making vindictive and cowardly men
into the monkeys and toads they already are

a ripple of coarse laughter spiced with jeers at the judges snakes through the room
as Anne Hutchinson now weak with hunger and near her time
gathers her spent body into a transcendent calm and utters the fatal words

              it came to me by direct revelation

this self-incrimination sends a whirlwind round and round the courtroom
as the magistrates pounce on this proof of Satan on her own tongue
instantly by unanimous vote they condemn her for all time in Massachusetts

that Mistress Hutchinson being convicted for traducing the ministers and their ministry
declared voluntarily her revelations thereupon she should be delivered

to her keeper Mr. Welde until the Court shall dispose of her by banishment

Mr. Cotton then speaks to the sisters of the church and advises them
to take heed of her opinions and to withhold all countenance and respect for her
lest they should harden her in her sin

      3.

like swaddling grave-clothes winter hardens New England
amid the tears of her children Anne Hutchinson stands in quiet dignity
to be excommunicated at which she turns her spirit toward the wilderness

I take this guilt into my heart that I am among the silenced ones
touched by Anne Hutchinson whose works earned heaven countless times
but who commended that power to God's grace alone

I take this guilt into my heart that I directly receive revelation
from the Scripture readings that I know not by brain alone
and for this I am heretic with Mistress Hutchinson though not so brave

I take this guilt into my heart that I nightly hear revelation sung
on the tongue of my Mistress wife of the magistrate who sleeps away
the paper nights when her poems appear for her working them into gold

So To Number Our Days

The twenty-fourth anniversary
of her birth has passed
and if the Dowager told me truth
mine as well

no note is taken
she spins and weaves and sews
endlessly silent but firm and motherly
a mistress and a servant both

yet some trouble stirs
within that still delicate white brow
an anguish or is this
the face of a pent captivity

in the stone-cold shed
by choice I huddle away from the hearth
shelling a heap of flint corn
until my grated thumbs go as numb

as the affrighted good-wives
in the aftermath of
the trial of Anne Hutchinson
what woman even a childless woman

can bear to eat or drink or feel
in her old human way now
that Anne Hutchinson and her children
wander at the mercy of wolves and blizzards

for speaking for speaking while
being a woman
well it is said somewhere by someone
that every angel terrifies

but does silent Anne Bradstreet wonder
how shall I so yearning to sing

live how shall I live
or shall I dumbly number my days

like the servant Meanwell
dully shelling kernel after kernel of flint
her downcast two-colored eyes
seeing only the terror that unites us

what will happen
to my unshelled poems of flint
will they be burnt with my body at the stake
or brought forth not at all

When the Ministers Heard Anne Hutchinson Was Scalped

At Ipswich time drizzles with ice rain
slipping towards the salt-ice sea
while each night Anne Bradstreet
writes out her blunted poems in secret
beside a sputtering pine-tar candle
with only the breathings of her little ones
warming the deserted bedstead

by daylight she is vigilant not to neglect
a single item of housewivery
and always to court the benign opinion
of that puffer the Reverend Nathaniel Ward
attending like a clockwork
all of his Sunday and Thursday meetings
and caring for his library books

thus I am with servants in the loft
of Ipswich church when a messenger
comes with tidings of Anne Hutchinson
how she'd spent some years
with Quaker heretics down in Pocasset
following the Inward Light
until they found offense in her too

whereupon widowed with children
she emigrated from the English altogether
to the Dutch at Pelham in Westchester
with her poor colony of sixteen
she assumed her simple belief in equal rights
for the Indians who owned the land
would grace her with their good will

it was said the Dutch had angered
Wampago who ruled the Pelham lands
it was said that during the massacre
Wampago himself scalped Anne Hutchinson
and all of her children but one

little Susanna with the bright red hair
who as captive was called Autumn Leaf

all the dying remains of Anne Hutchinson
the Indians hideously set ablaze
until not a trace of life stood where
house or human had been
but smoking timbers mangled about
among some charcoaled bones
and a foul smell of burnt bodies in the air

now the rain-soaked messenger pauses
for when the ministers heard Anne Hutchinson was scalped
the black-coates sent up a fearful yell
that might have been bloody savagery
but for Symme's scoffing at her misshapen child
and Wilson's roasting the American Jezebel
but not a female soul can speak

A Servant Drops a Lit Candle

But we must not remain in populous Ipswich
he says while it is still our duty to conquer
the wilderness in the name of our Puritan God
no pious man could in conscience do less
than strive for success and triumph and wealth
to be wrought from the savage land

to Cochichawicke we must chase the dream
of fertile farm-land fed by the Merrimack
he says and he does go and build his sawmill
to fashion their new house with great expense
and luxuries of walnut paneling and gables
and imported windows upon his twenty acres

that he calls Andover to slough a savage sound
where he will grow richer still on his mill
but struggling through tangles of bristling wood
heavy with her sixth child does she question
his acquisitiveness that sets her down in lavish
isolation from Ward's twittering library voice

she is obedient not like her wild sister Sarah
who defies men to their faces most of all
her husband Woodbridge divorced a cuckold
and Dudley is so bent on saving face he presses
them to publish Anne's chubby little book
as *The Tenth Muse Lately Sprung Up in America*

odd-cloaked as a muse she tends her wilderness
mansion filled with English chests and tables
and ancestral portraits and eight-hundred books
all of an Englishness I am meant to polish well
and preserve for those whose kind benevolence
allows me to grow old in service to this house

and I do polish and scrub here for twenty years
as she grows to love her nest feathered with things
that make her heart glad her husband her children
her writings on stashes of paper her vast hearth
her great baskets of carded sheep's wool that catch
the house afire when a servant drops a lit candle

EARTH

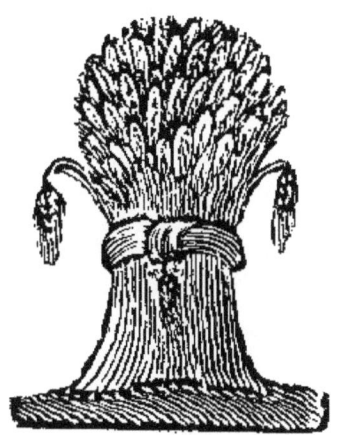

Sagamore

In smoking ruins Anne Bradstreet weeps
like the ghost of that other one
whose heart was blackened and broken by fire
but limping lame and twisted in body now
she grieves once for her pleasant things in ashes
then blesses the God who gave and took

however with the perseverance of her husband
who orders and purchases and oversees
a dozen carpenters the house is whole again
and litigious Simon Bradstreet turns his mind
to his right to sue his neighbors over this and that
an aggravating occupation but it keeps him home

for loosing his mare he sues the witless boy
indentured to his brother-in-law Sam Dudley
once his own pupil and for the running off
and slaughter of three swine he brings a case
against three swarthy Indian Pennacook men
seen lately taking alewives from Roger's Brook

chief Cutshamache makes his braves give up
a pelt or two in recompense but feelings go bad
to worse so when we walk one bleak midwinter day
in falling snow to the meetinghouse in the wood
to thank our Puritan God for His making good
the burnt-out house we walk with guns in a band

as the devil would have it Sam's ailing wife Mercy
leaves behind her psalter undiscovered till we are
halfway home and so I am told to quick fly back
for her little book alone which I do and find safe
where Mercy sat but meanwhile the glum afternoon
light has lain down amongst the leafless trees

as I venture toward the settlement again all alone
it is best not to think too much I think to myself
when I see the flash of scarlet tips on the snow
white feathers pinned in a threesome spray onto
the shrieking ram against my person yanking off
my stiff cap like to yank out all my loose gray hairs

but something in me rises pumping up unknown
strength through my long arms so that I throttle
the beast and throw him down and take a hold on
his hammer so as to meet the next one's attack
swinging and bashing the mark until the unearthly
shrill of strange words breaks the savage deviltry

that encircles me a crazed and swaying bear at bay
until Cutshamache himself the Pennacook sagamore
appears in his scarlet-tipped feather head-dress
shoves back my wild hair and meets my furious glare
puts his thumb first to the blue then to the brown
and in a dying light mutters in English *sky* and *earth*

the grim trees withdraw all trace of human otherness
I find myself alone on a scuff of beaten snow
I gather my hair into a hank and shove on my cap
I retrieve Mercy's half-split psalter from frozen waste
I hurry toward the settlement under my own power
as the rough thrust of native hands inflames my skin

Sister Death

The marvel is
that I have not seen God
in the growth of my enormous frame
and my flinten muscles
until

I fought the dark
animal in a half-lit forest
to protect and save I knew not what
except that it be
my life

how came I
suddenly to discover this
world of being braided and entwined
of body and soul
my life

stark alive
I find the heart to see
her cruel diminishment by pitiless years
and bodily pain while I am
magnified

mystery
how lame she bore
eight babes and labored as a cripple
her whole life her love
poem

now aching
my arms gather her swollen
near bloodless form from its spewn bed
and wash my sister death
for her grave

Of Husbands and Step-Dames

Bitter the sun cracked open light
that slopped over a sty
of lives left-over from adventure
across this vale before the perennial

weary weary that a man must look upon
servants doing what once was
the work of his wife in her constancy
and afterwards sleep alone

who will serve him and obey him
down to the smallest kiss of his most
unspeakable manly part
bewildering this empty vessel a house

children amounting to a pack of litters
grown half-grown barely grown
grand-children but a distant whine and saw
architects of nothing

so I have watched old Dudley think
and wait four months to take a willing wife
so I watch stodgy Bradstreet at seventy-three
four years after court the widow Gardner

yes I am old and I have seen it all
how step-dames ascend to imperial queenship
by executing dead first wives
and aborting their children from men's minds

they freshen with new offspring
that engross all houseroom and inheritance
this is reality but am I bound to serve it
this dread-hell she suffered when on earth

am I bound to serve what I hate

Two Annes Have I Served Half-Faithfully

Her chubby little book
lies still in its coffin of cherry wood
the spindly desk bought after the house-fire
though much was lost
much remains in sheaves of parchment
covered in her plain hand

her hands
a scholar's tender fingers
how could such smallness pour forth a thing
so mysterious as
        a poem   a book

no one goes there now
but I   I who once wished only to hate her
because she was loved by a mother
and doted on by a father
while I was made to be her servant
little Meanwell
who grew and grew like an ox

now only Meanwell snatches time to read
what is left
her epitaphs on too many babes
her upons upon her son Samuel her daughter Hannah
her dear and loving husband
her meditations in solitude
sneaking to read I remember how the soil
of bleeding garden beets
once traced lines in her hand

       *   *   *

Of the other her mind was laid bare
to all the ages hence
when Wampago sliced and ripped her scalp
I wonder did he see
what flitted away in the dark

from under the length of gray-black hair

once I heard her proclaim
that to be a woman was to be
blessed

that to be a woman was to possess mastery
of one's own
        body   one's own
                    mind

I confess I was afraid
as if the Holy Ghost had descended upon
weak humans and what were we
to do with the call to
        was it
a call to revolution   to defy a biblical
                interpretation

was not Eve the cause of all women's suffering
        and not men
was not Adam designed by God
        for mastery

I confess
I was afraid

still I am haunted by
        those fires of compassion
                that branded my soul in her embrace

        *   *   *

What I was to either Anne is not a mote of dust
perhaps   Bradstreet or Hutchinson
there is no way of grasping
the corpse of the past
without that it contaminates
the present hand with ghoulish masquerade

lump of clay that I am
neither gifted with the voice of the poet
nor the voice of the freedom fighter
it is enough to remember
and go on
well

In Exile from Grave Illusion

When I do think when I do think
I do think that
        the thinking may be all
my goods in America

my goods my bare corner of duds

one brown bodice
one brown skirt
one undyed under-dress
one mended bonnet
one vast woolen cloak stitched-over from two cloaks
one pair of broken-buckled man's shoes
a wad of small-clothes

cast-offs of Puritan prosperity   moth-eaten

when I think to look at myself
        now
in passages of pond-water and pond-ice
I do ponder before
I have to laugh
            at what's become of
    me

how forty-years of wondering in America
have produced this mean old
        giantess

thank God that Guy de Poingdestre from Jersey
that silver-tongued Frenchy cow-man cannot see this
but what if he should
even now thrive in Carteret's lush new Jersey
it would serve him more than well
for what a fool I was
to believe   to believe
rhymes with Eve so what if those
ministers may be right

no I believe
        with two Annes
it is blessed to be
woman

Meanwell

Ruined as I was and nameless in the beginning
I came to believe that I sprang
from nothing
                  and was bound to end
in nothing
      for my soul if I possessed
such a one
         a twin it would appear
to my body   could only manifest itself as
         a whelpless wounded she-bear

unnatural   or too devilish a wild nature

it seemed fitting that I serve
that I should be made a servant to a finer
creation of God
                but now I cry why has God also
created me   was it only for my ruin
for a life of penance and ignorance

errant soul I wonder now at your largesse
        in my dearth of time
I touch you in the sprawl of my body
how immense you have grown
        in America
after forty years   you are unbuckling out of yourself
you are prepared at last to throw off
your chains   nothing remains to require
your servitude or your tenderness
your standing and waiting

I speak to myself in the shadow
of the darkened house of Anne Bradstreet that was
and shoulder my pack of goods
        Meanwell
though often I did fail
                  in England and Massachusetts

now through brown and blue
I search the dim snow before sunrise
for the moment I make tracks

through bare listening trees

        Westward

Fomite
Burlington, Vermont

Fomite is a literary press whose authors and artists explore the human condition -- political, cultural, personal and historical -- in poetry and prose.

A fomite is a medium capable of transmitting infectious organisms from one individual to another.

"The activity of art is based on the capacity of people to be infected by the feelings of others." Tolstoy, *What is Art?*

AlphaBetaBestiario - Antonello Borra
Animals have always understood that mankind is not fully at home in the world. Bestiaries, hoping to teach, send out warnings. This one, of course, aims at doing the same.

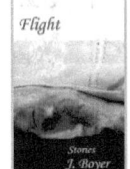

Flight and Other Stories - Jay Boyer
In *Flight and Other Stories,* we're with the fattest woman on earth as she draws her last breaths and her soul ascends toward its final reward. We meet a divorcee who can fly for no more effort than flapping her arms. We follow a middle-aged butler whose love affair with a young woman leads him first to the mysteries of bondage, and then to the pleasures of malice. Story by story, we set foot into worlds so strange as to seem all but surreal, yet everything feels familiar, each moment rings true. And that's when we recognize we're in the hands of one of America's truly original talents.

Improvisational Arguments - Anna Faktorovich
Improvisational Arguments is written in free verse to capture the essence of modern problems and triumphs. The poems clearly relate short, frequently humorous and occasionally tragic, stories about travels to exotic and unusual places, fantastic realms, abnormal jobs, artistic innovations, political objections, and misadventures with love.

Loisaida - Dan Chodorokoff
Catherine, a young anarchist estranged from her parents and squatting in an abandoned building on New York's Lower East Side is fighting with her boyfriend and conflicted about her work on an underground newspaper. After learning of a developer's plans to demolish a community garden, Catherine builds an alliance with a group of Puerto Rican community activists. Together they confront the confluence of politics, money, and real estate that rule Manhattan. All the while she learns important lessons from her great-grandmother's life in the Yiddish anarchist movement that flourished on the Lower East Side at the turn of the century. In this coming of age story, family saga, and tale of urban politics, Dan Chodorkoff explores the "principle of hope", and examines how memory and imagination inform social change.

Fomite
Burlington, Vermont

Still Time - Michael Cocchiarale

Still Time is a collection of twenty-five short and shorter stories exploring tensions that arise in a variety of contemporary relationships: a young boy must deal with the wrath of his out-of-work father; a woman runs into a man twenty years after an awkward sexual encounter; a wife, unable to conceive, imagines her own murder, as well as the reaction of her emotionally distant husband; a soon-to-be tenured English professor tries to come to terms with her husband's shocking return to the religion of his youth; an assembly line worker, married for thirty years, discovers the surprising secret life of his recently hospitalized wife. Whether a few hundred or a few thousand words, these and other stories in the collection depict characters at moments of deep crisis. Some feel powerless, overwhelmed—unable to do much to change the course of their lives. Others rise to the occasion and, for better or for worse, say or do the thing that might transform them for good. Even in stories with the most troubling of endings, there remains the possibility of redemption. For each of the characters, there is still time.

Loosestrife - Greg Delanty

This book is a chronicle of complicity in our modern lives, a witnessing of war and the destruction of our planet. It is also an attempt to adjust the more destructive blueprint myths of our society. Often our cultural memory tells us to keep quiet about the aspects that are most challenging to our ethics, to forget the violations we feel and tremors that keep us distant and numb.

Carts and Other Stories - Zdravka Evtimova

Roots and wings are the key words that best describe the short story collection, *Carts and Other Stories*, by Zdravka Evtimova. The book is emotionally multilayered and memorable because of its internal power, vitality and ability to touch both the heart and your mind. Within its pages, the reader discovers new perspectives true wealth, and learns to see the world with different eyes. The collection lives on the borders of different cultures. *Carts and Other Stories* will take the reader to wild and powerful Bulgarian mountains, to silver rains in Brussels, to German quiet winter streets and to wind bitten crags in Afghanistan. This book lives for those seeking to discover the beauty of the world around them, and will have them appreciating what they have— and perhaps what they have lost as well.

The Listener Aspires to the Condition of Music - Barry Goldensohn

"I know of no other selected poems that selects on one theme, but this one does, charting Goldensohn's career-long attraction to music's performance, consolations and its august, thrilling, scary and clownish charms. Does all art aspire to the condition of music as Pater claimed, exhaling in a swoon toward that one class act? Goldensohn is more aware than the late 19th century of the overtones of such breathing: his poems thoroughly round out those overtones in a poet's lifetime of listening."
John Peck, poet, editor, Fellow of the American Academy of Rome

The Co-Conspirator's Tale - Ron Jacobs

There's a place where love and mistrust are never at peace; where duplicity and deceit are the universal currency. *The Co-Conspirator's Tale* takes place within this nebulous firmament. There are crimes committed by the police in the name of the law. Excess in the name of revolution. The combination leaves death in its wake and the survivors struggling to find justice in a San Francisco Bay Area noir by the author of the underground classic *The Way the Wind Blew: A History of the Weather Underground* and the novel *Short Order Frame Up*.

Fomite
Burlington, Vermont

When You Remember Deir Yassin - R.L Green

When You Remember Deir Yassin is a collection of poems by R. L. Green, an American Jewish writer, on the subject of the occupation and destruction of Palestine. Green comments: "Outspoken Jewish critics of Israeli crimes against humanity have, strangely, been called 'anti-Semitic' as well as the hilariously illogical epithet 'self-hating Jews.' As a Jewish critic of the Israeli government, I have come to accept these accusations as a stamp of approval and a badge of honor, signifying my own fealty to a central element of Jewish identity and ethics: one must be a lover of truth and a friend to the oppressed, and stand with the victims of tyranny, not with the tyrants, despite tribal loyalty or self-advancement. These poems were written as expressions of outrage, and of grief, and to encourage my sisters and brothers of every cultural or national grouping to speak out against injustice, to try to save Palestine, and in so doing, to reclaim for myself my own place as part of the Jewish people." Poems in the original English are accompanied by Arabic and Hebrew translations.

Roadworthy Creature, Roadworthy Craft - Kate Magill

Words fail but the voice struggles on. The culmination of a decade's worth of performance poetry, *Roadworthy Creature, Roadworthy Craft* is Kate Magill's first full-length publication. In lines that are sinewy yet delicate, Magill's poems explore the terrain where idea and action meet, where bodies and words commingle to form a strange new flesh, a breathing text, an "I" that spirals outward from itself.

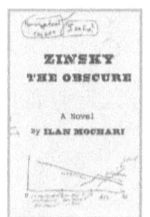

Zinsky the Obscure - Ilan Mochari

"If your childhood is brutal, your adulthood becomes a daily attempt to recover: a quest for ecstasy and stability in recompense for their early absence." So states the 30-year-old Ariel Zinsky, whose bachelor-like lifestyle belies the torturous youth he is still coming to grips with. As a boy, he struggles with the beatings themselves; as a grownup, he struggles with the world's indifference to them. *Zinsky the Obscure* is his life story, a humorous chronicle of his search for a redemptive ecstasy through sex, an entrepreneurial sports obsession, and finally, the cathartic exercise of writing it all down. Fervently recounting both the comic delights and the frightening horrors of a life in which he feels – always – that he is not like all the rest, Zinsky survives the worst and relishes the best with idiosyncratic style, as his heartbreak turns into self-awareness and his suicidal ideation into self-regard. A vivid evocation of the all-consuming nature of lust and ambition – and the forces that drive them.

Love's Labours - Jack Pulaski

In the four stories and two novellas that comprise *Love's Labors* the protagonists Ben and Laura, discover in their fervid romance and long marriage their interlocking fates, and the histories that preceded their births. They also learned something of the paradox between love and all the things it brings to its beneficiaries: bliss, disaster, duty, tragedy, comedy, the grotesque, and tenderness.

Ben and Laura's story is also the particularly American tale of immigration to a new world. Laura's story begins in Puerto Rico, and Ben's lineage is Russian-Jewish. They meet in City College of New York, a place at least analogous to a melting pot. Laura struggles to rescue her brother from gang life and heroin. She is mother to her younger sister; their mother Consuelo is the financial mainstay of the family and consumed by work. Despite filial obligations, Laura aspires to be a serious painter. Ben writes, cares for and is caught up in the misadventures and surreal stories of his younger schizophrenic brother. Laura is also a story teller as powerful and enchanting as Scheherazade.

Ben struggles to survive such riches, and he and Laura endure.

Fomite
Burlington, Vermont

The Derivation of Cowboys & Indians - Joseph D. Reich

The Derivation of Cowboys & Indians represents a profound journey, a breakdown of The American Dream from a social, cultural, historical, and spiritual point of view. Reich examines in concise!detail the loss of the collective unconscious, commenting on our!contemporary postmodern culture with its self-interested excesses, on where and how things all go wrong, and how social/political practice rarely meets its original proclamations and promises. Reich's surreal and self-effacing satire brings this troubling message home. *The Derivations of Cowboys & Indians* is a desperate search and struggle for America's literal, symbolic, and spiritual home.

Kasper Planet: Comix and Tragix - Peter Schumann

The British call him Punch, the Italians, Pulchinello, the Russians, Petruchka, the Native Americans, Coyote. These are the figures we may know. But every culture that worships authority will breed a Punch-like, anti-authoritan resister. Yin and yang -- it has to happen. The Germans call him Kasper. Truth-telling and serious pranking are dangerous professions when going up against power. Bradley Manning sits naked in solitary; Julian Assange is pursued by Interpol, Obama's Department of Justice, and Amazon.com. But -- in contrast to merely human faces -- masks and theater can often slip through the bars. Consider our American Kaspers: Charlie Chaplin, Woody Guthrie, Abby Hoffman, the Yes Men -- theater people all, utilizing various forms to seed critique. Their profiles and tactics have evolved along with those of their enemies. Who are the bad guys that call forth the Kaspers? Over the last half century, with his Bread & Puppet Theater, Peter Schumann has been tireless in naming them, excoriating them with Kasperdom....
from Marc Estrin's Foreword to Planet Kasper

Views Cost Extra - *L.E. Smith*

Views that inspire, that calm, or that terrify – all come at some cost to the viewer. In *Views Cost Extra* you will find a New Jersey high school preppy who wants to inhabit the "perfect" cowboy movie, a rural mailman disgusted with the residents of his town who wants to live with the penguins, an ailing screen writer who strikes a deal with Johnny Cash to reverse an old man's failures, an old man who ponders a young man's suicide attempt, a one-armed blind blues singer who wants to reunite with the car that took her arm on the assembly line -- and more. These stories suggest that we must pay something to live even ordinary lives.

The Empty Notebook Interrogates Itself - Susan Thomas

The Empty Notebook began its life as a very literal metaphor for a few weeks of what the poet thought was writer's block, but was really the struggle of an eccentric persona to take over her working life. It won. And for the next three years everything she wrote came to her in the voice of the Empty Notebook, who, as the notebook began to fill itself, became rather opinionated, changed gender, alternately acted as bully and victim, had many bizarre adventures in exotic locales and developed a somewhat politically-incorrect attitude. It then began to steal the voices and forms of other poets and tried to immortalize itself in various poetry reviews. It is now thrilled to collect itself in one slim volume.

Fomite
Burlington, Vermont

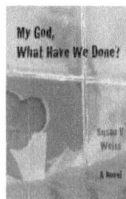

My God, What Have We Done? - Susan Weiss

In a world afflicted with war, toxicity, and hunger, does what we do in our private lives really matter? Fifty years after the creation of the atomic bomb at Los Alamos, newlyweds Pauline and Clifford visit that once-secret city on their honeymoon, compelled by Pauline's fascination with Oppenheimer, the soulful scientist. The two stories emerging from this visit reverberate back and forth between the loneliness of a new mother at home in Boston and the isolation of an entire community dedicated to the development of the bomb. While Pauline struggles with unforeseen challenges of family life, Oppenheimer and his crew reckon with forces beyond all imagining.

Finally the years of frantic research on the bomb culminate in a stunning test explosion that echoes a rupture in the couple's marriage. Against the backdrop of a civilization that's out of control, Pauline begins to understand the complex, potentially explosive physics of personal relationships.

At once funny and dead serious, *My God, What Have We Done?* sifts through the ruins left by the bomb in search of a more worthy human achievement.

As It Is On Earth - Peter M. Wheelwright

Four centuries after the Reformation Pilgrims sailed up the down-flowing watersheds of New England, Taylor Thatcher, irreverent scion of a fallen family of Maine Puritans, is still caught in the turbulence.

In his errant attempts to escape from history, the young college professor is further unsettled by his growing attraction to Israeli student Miryam Bluehm as he is swept by Time through the "family thing" – from the tangled genetic and religious history of his New England parents to the redemptive birthday secret of Esther Fleur Noire Bishop, the Cajun-Passamaquoddy woman who raised him and his younger half-cousin/half-brother, Bingham.

The landscapes, rivers, and tidal estuaries of Old New England and the Mayan Yucatan are also casualties of history in Thatcher's story of Deep Time and re-discovery of family on Columbus Day at a high-stakes gambling casino, rising in resurrection over the starlit bones of a once-vanquished Pequot Indian Tribe.

Travers' Inferno - *L.E. Smith*

In the 1970's churches began to burn in Burlington, Vermont. If it were arson, no one or no reason could be found to blame. This book suggests arson, but makes no claim to historical realism. It claims, instead, to capture the dizzying 70's zeitgeist of aggressive utopian movements, distrust in authority, escapist alternative life styles, and a bewildered society of onlookers. In the tradition of John Gardner's Sunlight Dialogues, the characters of *Travers' Inferno* are colorful and damaged, sometimes comical, sometimes tragic, looking for meaning through desperate acts. Travers Jones, protagonist, is grounded in the transcendent – philosophy, epilepsy, arson as purification – and mystified by the opposite sex, haunted by an absent father and directed by an uncle with a grudge. He is seduced by a professor's wife and chased by an endearing if ineffective sergeant of police. There are secessionist Quebecois involved in these church burns who are murdering as well as pilfering and burning. There are changing alliances, violent deaths, lovemaking, and a belligerent cat.

Fomite
Burlington, Vermont

Visiting Hours - *Jennider Anne Moses*
Visiting Hours, a novel-in-stories, explores the lives of people not normally met on the page---AIDS patients and those who care for them. Set in Baton Rouge, Louisiana, and written with large and frequent dollops of humor, the book is a profound meditation on faith and love in the face of illness and poverty.

Suite for Three Voices - *Derek Furr*
Suite for Three Voices is a dance of prose genres, teeming with intense human life in all its humor and sorrow. A son uncovers the horrors of his father's wartime experience, a hitchhiker in a muumuu guards a mysterious parcel, a young man foresees his brother's brush with death on September 11. A Victorian poetess encounters space aliens and digital archives, a runner hears the voice of a dead friend in the song of an indigo bunting, a teacher seeks wisdom from his students' errors and Neil Young. By frozen waterfalls and neglected graveyards, along highways at noon and rivers at dusk, in the sound of bluegrass, Beethoven, and Emily Dickinson, the essays and fiction in this collection offer moments of vision.

The Good Muslim of Jackson Heights - *Jaysinh Birjépatil*
Jackson Heights in this book is a fictional locale with common features assembled from immigrant-friendly neighborhoods around the world where hardworking honest-to-goodness traders from the Indian subcontinent, rub shoulders with ruthless entrepreneurs, reclusive antique-dealers, homeless nobodies, merchant-princes, lawyers, doctors and IT specialists. But as Siraj and Shabnam, urbane newcomers fleeing religious persecution in their homeland discover there is no escape from the past. Weaving together the personal and the political *The Good Muslim of Jackson Heights* is an ambiguous elegy to a utopian ideal set free from all prejudice.

Did you know that you can write a review on Amazon, Good Reads or Shelfari? Just go to the book page on the website and follow the links for posting a review. Independent presses rely on reader to reader communication to grow audiences for our authors and their books.